IRISH LONDONERS

PHOTOGRAPHS FROM THE PADDY FAHEY COLLECTION

FINBARR WHOOLEY

Foreword by the Irish Ambassador Edward Barrington

GRANGE MUSEUM

SUTTON PUBLISHING LIMITED

Sutton Publishing Limited
Phoenix Mill · Thrupp · Stroud
Gloucestershire · GL5 2BU

First published 1997

Title page: Young and old out on the floor at a
Clan Connacht social evening, 1965.

British Library Cataloguing in Publication Data
A catalogue record for this book is available from the
British Library.

ISBN 0-7509-1371-1

Typeset in 10/12 Perpetua.
Typesetting and origination by
Sutton Publishing Limited.
Printed in Great Britain by
Ebenezer Baylis, Worcester.

Acknowledgements

I wish to thank the following: Danny Aherne, Ambassador Ted Barrington, Fr Denis Cormican OMI, William Carson, Marion Cooper, Kathryn O'Connell, my colleagues at Cricklewood Library and Archive, Kate Dempsey, Meadbh Dempsey, Tom Dunne, Peggy Fahey, Pat Griffin, Fr Bill Hanley, Bridget Keane, Michael Keane, Mary Kenny, Geoffrey Keating, Finbarr Lehane, Margaret Lehane, Patrick Lynch, Bill Mawn, Julie Rajakoul, Marie Ryan, Marion Savage, Pat St George, Fachtna Whooley, Tom Wyse, and my colleagues at the Grange Museum, Shereen Harrack-Singh, Nick Lane, Joy Price and Alex Sidney.

Dedicated to the memory of Paddy Fahey

CONTENTS

A view of the mineral bar at the Blarney Club, Tottenham Court Road, early 1950s.

FOREWORD

It is a real pleasure to welcome Finbarr Whooley's *Irish Londoners,* which brings together some of the most interesting photographs from the Paddy Fahey Archive and which chronicles the life and development of the Irish community in London from 1950 to 1980. The photographs capture in a compelling way the range of personalities in the Irish community and the social events which shaped their lives. It is a fascinating record of the period and is redolent of the atmosphere of the times. It is also a record of change and adaptation and illustrates the way in which the Irish community could retain a sense of a distinct identity while participating in the life of London.

I was privileged to be present at the opening of the exhibition of photographs from the Fahey Archive in March 1996 at the Grange Museum in Neasden. I was conscious then of witnessing a significant record of the Irish experience in Britain, and at the same time an important record of English social history, for it is impossible to imagine the development of London without the contribution made by generations of Irish men and women. The Fahey exhibition has since then gone on to visit many centres in Ireland and it is surely appropriate that the experience of the Irish in London should be commemorated in Ireland as well as in Britain.

I am delighted that the Cultural Relations Committee of Ireland and the Ireland Fund of Great Britain helped to conserve the Fahey Archive. We are in Finbarr Whooley's debt for his achievement in preserving these photographs and for his efforts to make them better known.

This is a book which will have an appeal beyond the Irish community in Britain. It will fascinate all those who appreciate the diversity of London life and the complexity of its social fabric. In the faces reproduced in these pages are marked the hopes and the experiences of an immigrant people who with hard work, determination and humour made their lives here. In these faces there is a remarkable and inspiring story.

Edward Barrington
Ambassador

INTRODUCTION

Irish people have lived in London in significant numbers since the eighteenth century. Over the years specific areas of the capital became associated with the community, such as Seven Dials in Covent Garden in the nineteenth century and Camden Town and Kilburn in the twentieth. Since Victorian times there has been a constant trickle of Irish emigration to London. At times when economic depression in Ireland or denial of easy access to other countries such as the USA offered no other opportunities to young Irish people that trickle turned into a flood. Whatever the numbers, however, there always remained a significant community in London, which could offer a fresh start to later generations of emigrants.

London represented an economic bolt-hole from poverty in Ireland. It was near and relatively cheap to get to. There was work to be had for those who had no difficulty with hard physical labour and there were plenty of other Irish people in London to welcome the emigrant upon arrival.

Although emigration to London had occurred over a long period, it reached its highest level for a century in the 1950s. Deep economic depression in Ireland led to a massive haemorrhage of the population. The 1950s Diaspora completely defined the nature of London Irish life from that point onwards. By the early 1960s London really was Ireland's thirty-third county.

The society that Paddy Fahey photographed in the 1950s and '60s was a vibrant and self-contained one. Like all such communities, the Irish emigrants to London in the postwar period sought little from the city except an opportunity to find work. All the other structures of community life, from welfare provision to accommodation, were largely undertaken by the community itself. The role of the Catholic Church was crucial in these areas. Irish priests travelled to London to minister to the community, and helped build churches and schools. They were involved in general welfare provision and in housing matters. As was the case in Ireland, the Church wasn't compartmentalized and separate from other aspects of life. Almost everyone shared a basic belief and they looked to the priest as a natural leader and recognized a role for the Church in all aspects of society.

The self-help ethos of the London Irish is epitomized by the growth of the county associations. From modest beginnings in the early 1950s, these associations flourished and took on an important role in providing social outlets for a cross-section of the community. They also sponsored welfare provision.

The role that the Irish Embassy played throughout the 1950s and '60s was also significant. The unfinished business between Ireland and Britain, which had dominated their relations since the 1920s, meant that the Irish Ambassador to London played a crucial role in implementing Irish government policy. A major plank of that policy in the 1950s was the work of the Anti-Partition League, a pan-Nationalist movement established by Taoiseach John A. Costello in 1947. The national question was a live issue. The generation who fought the Anglo-Irish War were still in power in Ireland and prominent in all fields of Irish life both in Ireland and among the Irish Diaspora. There was always the danger of old conflicts exploding again, as they did during the IRA border campaign of 1959–61.

In this context one would think that the welfare of ordinary Irish emigrants would not have been a major priority for Embassy staff. However, their sheer numbers meant that they could not be ignored.

Just as the Catholic Church responded to the new immigration so too did the Embassy, and during the tenure of Ambassador Boland appeared to take a greater interest in ordinary Irish immigrants than had been the case before.

Throughout the period covered by this book the Gaelic Athletic Association (GAA) played a major role in London Irish life. Probably the oldest Irish institution in London, the GAA gave support to young Irish people, helped build a sense of community and provided entertainment for the London Irish. It was also linked via a complex series of personal relationships with the county associations, the construction industry and employment generally, and to political organizations like the Old IRA.

Irish Londoners came together in large numbers after mass on Sundays, at football matches, at large annual celebrations like St Patrick's Day and most famously at dancehalls. There was a long history of Irish dancehalls in London stretching back to before the Second World War. Unlike pubs, the dancehalls offered a neutral venue for both sexes. Dancehalls were centres where young Irish people could meet, exchange news from home and listen to football matches as well as dance.

It was in this society that Paddy Fahey plied his trade. In 1941 Paddy arrived in London from his native County Waterford. At the time of his arrival in England he was a qualified photographer, having worked extensively for many Irish newspapers over the previous decade. Like many recent immigrants, however, Paddy was not initially able to work at his chosen profession and found employment as a labourer instead.

Within a few years he was again working as a full-time photographer. Much of his newspaper work involved documenting the everyday life of the emerging postwar Irish community. Over thirty years he was a familiar figure at all Irish events, from official functions at the Irish Embassy to sporting, religious and cultural activities. Paddy withdrew from press photography in the 1970s, but he continued to work as a studio photographer until his death in 1994.

Paddy Fahey photographed many aspects of London Irish life. However, there were also things that he did not photograph. He was a freelance photographer working for editors who needed lots of faces in order to sell newspapers. Thus Paddy rarely photographed the community at work. Neither did he photograph some of its more unpleasant aspects – poverty, homelessness or anti-Irish feeling. That was not a role that Paddy would have taken to even if his news assignments allowed him to do so. Paddy Fahey was like his contemporaries, a conservative man, and he knew instinctively when to take a photograph and when to hold back. His work was not that of an outsider looking in, but rather of an insider photographing his own.

This book has evolved over many years. In 1992 I was introduced to Paddy by Bernard Canavan. Paddy generously showed me his photo archive and from that time we were determined to save the collection for posterity. Unfortunately Paddy died in 1994 and it was Paddy's widow Peggy to whom we eventually turned. Peggy very kindly passed on Paddy's collection to the Grange Museum. With generous assistance from the Ireland Fund of Great Britain and the Foreign Affairs Committee of the Department of Irish Foreign Affairs, we were able to conserve his pictures. There are over 5,000 images in the Paddy Fahey Archive, which is housed at Cricklewood Library and Archive.

Over the past months I have spent a lot of time in conversation with Paddy's contemporaries in an effort to match faces with names. Undoubtedly some incorrect names will pass through the net and for that I apologize in advance. However, I would urge anyone with more information on the images in the book to contact me and I will endeavour to correct my errors in any future publications.

OURSELVES ALONE

*A large banner proclaiming the Limerick Association is displayed outside government offices at Whitehall.
The annual St Patrick's Day march by the county associations through Whitehall became an established
feature of London Irish life in the 1950s. In the front row, third and fourth from left, are Mr Noonan and
Tom O'Donnell.*

There was little in the way of help from the state for the recently arrived emigrant, so the burden of this work fell on the community itself. In the 1950s many self-help initiatives were originated by the London Irish. The county associations, founded in the early 1950s, played a very important role. Although they were social in nature, they were always charitable in intent. Members of county associations together with members of other groups such as the Legion of Mary often went to Euston to direct young emigrants to safe accommodation. Establishing hostels and safe digs was not easy. All moneys spent on these initiatives had to be raised by the community. Energetic and resourceful people like Fr McNamara, the Chaplain at the Camden Irish Centre, worked hard to create safe havens for the new emigrants.

The county associations organized outings for young and old, they ran popular annual dinner dances and in many other modest ways helped Irish people to mingle with their own. They helped to foster the informal but ultimately vital networks that assisted people to find jobs, accommodation and sometimes spouses in a strange land.

The self-help ethos extended to many aspects of London Irish life, from cultural to sporting activities, and Paddy Fahey's photographs taken throughout the 1950s and '60s are testament to this.

The inaugural meeting of the Council of Irish Counties was held at the Irish Club in Eaton Square. Front row, left to right: T. MacCavanagh (Armagh), J. Conway (Cavan), Frank Biggar (Irish Embassy), Eamonn O'Donnell (Donegal), Fr Tom McNamara, Dr Tom Tangney (Cork), Dr F. Boland, the Irish Ambassador, Dr J. Canning (Donegal), Fr Tom Moore (Cavan); Back row, from base of the stairs: Tadgh Feehan, Tony Murphy (Cork), Fr Cremin, Simon Breen (Tipperary), W. Gleeson (Limerick), Jack Stacey, Harry Bolger (Tipperary), J. Carr (Donegal), J. Moriarty, Paddy White (Kerry), J. McAvinchey (Armagh).

Women were well represented in all but name at this gathering of the Longford Men's Association, 1954. Women rarely featured in the many committees photographed by Paddy in the 1950s and '60s. However, it is worth noting that in this regard the London Irish were no different from their counterparts at home or their English neighbours.

In 1963 the county associations turned out in force for the annual St Patrick's Day march through Whitehall. Here the Wexfordmen file past Horseguards Parade. The St Patrick's Day marches continued throughout the 1960s until the outbreak of hostilities in Northern Ireland caused this outward display of Irishness in the capital to cease.

The Ambassador and the chairmen of the county associations at Camden Irish Centre, 1963. Before the foundation of the county associations there was little in the way of local organizations for the Irish in London. The associations consisted of a committee of about ten, and their purpose was to act as a social gathering point for people of their home counties, through organized events, benefits and galas. The constitution of the county associations from the outset was non-sectarian and non-political. Front row, left to right: Tadgh Feehan, Tom McGowan, Ambassador Con Cremin, Michael Quinn, Fr McNamara. Also present are Jerry O'Flynn from Galway (back row, third from right) and Sean McGill and Tom Wyse (second row, second and third from right).

Although the county associations were non-sectarian in constitution, in reality the vast majority of those who attended county association events were Catholic. London Irish society at the time was no different from 1950s Irish society, secular in name but deeply Catholic in reality. The sentiment expressed in the Sligo Association 'Faith of Our Fathers' banner was shared by most of the London Irish of the period. The occasion for this display of popular piety was the Sligo Association Dinner Dance in 1962. In the centre at the front is Tom Beckett, Chairman of the Sligo Association. Also present are Paddy Watters and Bert Hunt (second row, first and eighth from right).

The inaugural meeting of the Mayo Association, 1963. Those present include: Tom McGowan (back row, first left), John Ennis (back row, second right), Michael Quinn (front row, first left), who was chairman of the combined Irish counties associations, and Nancy Gallen (front row, second left), who together with her husband Gerry was host at the Enkel Arms pub, a popular music venue on Seven Sisters Road.

The growth of the county associations is a good indicator of the level of Irish emigration to London. By the early 1960s all of the major county associations had been established. This 1962 photograph records the annual general meeting of the Waterford Association. Those present include: Jim Fox (back row, first left), Paddy Whitty (second row, fifth left), Mrs Lehane (second row, seventh left), Jim Griffin (front row, first right), Secretary of the Waterford Association, and Willie Baron (front row, second right).

The annual dinner dance of the Galway Association held at the Casserley Court Hotel, 1966. The hotel was named after its owners the Casserley brothers from Galway and was situated off the Bayswater Road. Fr J. Casey, a member of the Columban Fathers, is seated in the centre of the picture.

The Donegal Men's dinner, 1952. Those present include Ambassador Boland and Mrs Boland (front row, third and fourth left) and Tadgh Feehan (standing, second right). Seated next to Ambassador Boland is Caher Healey. Also included are: Eileen Kilgallen, the Secretary of the Irish Club, Eaton Square, Dr Tom Tangney (back row, first and second left), and Fr Cremin from Kerry (back row, fourth right).

A meeting of the Wexford Association, early 1950s. The chairman was Tommy Quirke (front row, centre), and also present is Tommy Murphy (front row, second left).

The first annual Galway Association dinner dance, 1959. Left to right: Gerry O'Flynn, Eddie O'Connell, Joe Clarke, Fr Brendan Burke, Mrs Gleeson, Frank Biggar (councillor, Irish Embassy), Jack Gleeson, Dr Browne (Bishop of Galway). Jack Gleeson was a very important figure among the London Irish. As the owner of a large construction firm, he was responsible either directly or indirectly for the employment of hundreds of men.

A large group of people gathered for a joint dinner held by the Wexford and Tipperary Associations, late 1950s. Front row, left to right: Gerry O'Flynn, Kath Nicoll, Nell O'Flynn, Joseph Cunnane (Archbishop of Tuam), J.P. Gleeson, Mrs Rush, Kevin Rush, Bobby Molloy. Back row: May Quinn, Tommy O'Gorman, Jim Conway, Jim Mullerhy, Fr Sean Fay, Chris Hill, Michael Mullane, Fr J. Casey, Fr Brendan Burke, Mrs Mullen, Fr P. Hackett, Joe Clarke, Fr McNamara.

The Kilkenny Association organized a tribute to Fr Ronayne at the Irish Club, Eaton Square, early 1950s. Fr Ronayne had distinguished himself while a prisoner of the Japanese during the Second World War. He is seated at the front, second right, with members of his family. Tom Fitzgerald from the Irish Embassy is on his extreme left.

The United Ireland Association, 1967. The United Irish Association replaced the Anti-Partition League in 1964. Seated, left to right: Frank McCabe, John McCann, Jim Cummins, Paddy O'Connor, Eta Culleton, Tadgh Feehan. Second row: Mrs Conway, John Vaughan, Mrs O'Neill, Michael Casey, Ben Ennis, Clive Woodhouse, William Loftus, Mick Brown, Michael Dennehy.

When the John F. Kennedy Memorial Hall in the Camden Irish Centre was built in 1964 it was the Gleeson construction firm that undertook the work. Self-made Irish businessmen like Jack Gleeson (front, centre) often took on roles as natural figureheads and feature throughout Paddy Fahey's photographs. The picture also includes Dominic Donnelly, Roscommon (front, left) and Mick Casey (front, right).

The county associations organized many social events, and group outings were always popular. This outing of the Corkmen's Association set out from The Lord High Admiral. The Lord High Admiral was run by Paddy Whitty and was a great meeting place for the Irish community. The photograph includes Michael O'Brien (centre, wearing a hat) and Tim Howard, Secretary of the Cork Association (third from O'Brien's left).

Waterford Association outing, late 1950s. It is not known where this photograph was taken, but the picnic bags, buckets and spades and summer dresses suggest a trip to the seaside. The summer outings were always to popular resorts such as Margate and Brighton.

Following the appointment of John Molloy as the new Irish Ambassador the Committee of Irish Societies hosted a reception in his honour at the Irish Centre at Eaton Square, 1964. Left to right: John Brady (Treasurer), Tommy O'Gorman (President), Jack Molloy (Irish Ambassador), Jim Conway (Chairman) and Tom Wyse (Secretary). Between them Tommy O'Gorman and Jim Conway controlled some of the most popular dancing venues in London – Tommy ran the Gresham on the Holloway Road and Jim the Emerald in Hammersmith.

The meal over and the dancing yet to begin, a typical dinner-dance scene at the Kildare Association's annual dinner dance, 1968. Annual dinner dances were staged in the winter around Christmas.

Members of the Roscommon Association at the Irish Centre, Camden, 1958. The front row includes Mary Kenny (second left), Ann Kenny (third left) and Tommy Gillern (extreme right). In the back row are Eileen Gillern (third left) and Dominic Donnelly (extreme right).

Members of the organizing committee of the Camden Irish Centre. Front row, left to right: Fr McNamara (Chaplain to the Irish Centre), Monsignor Derek Worlock (later Bishop of Liverpool), Dominic Donnelly and Frank Pakenham (later Lord Longford), Michael Casey and Tadgh Feehan. The back row includes Paddy Keegan (second left), Dr Matt Cranitch and John Vaughan (first and second right).

In 1963 Wembley Arena was crowded with members of the Irish community in London for the screening of *The Day of Dreams*, a film about the life of John F. Kennedy. Attendance at the event included the American Envoy. From this period onwards the dead President Kennedy assumed an almost saint-like reputation among the Irish population both in Ireland and among the Irish Diaspora.

The 1964 Cavan Association Dinner was held under the famous backdrop of O'Connell Street at the Gresham Ballroom, Holloway Road.

This gathering of community leaders in 1963 was planned to establish a memorial to J.F. Kennedy. The combined areas of knowledge and interest of this group included the Old IRA, the GAA, the entertainment world, the county associations and the Catholic Church. The photograph includes, in the front row: Fr Burke, Fr McNamara, Dominic Donnelly, J.P. Gleeson, Michael Casey; in the back row: John Vaughan, Dr Cranitch, Tom Wyse, Dr Larry Morton, Jim Conway, Paddy Clifford, John Brady, John Geraghty, Jerry O'Flynn, Sean McGill.

The clergy are well represented at this gathering of the London Irish for the opening of the New Emerald Club, Hammersmith, 1951. The clergy were an integral part of all community events at this time. Their presence was usually actively encouraged. In that sense the community of the London Irish was a carbon copy of 1950s Irish society, where the clergy played a pivotal role in all aspects of life.

Two photographs spanning a career. The top picture features the Southwark Cathedral Rebuilding Committee from the 1950s. At the front left of the photograph is Tadgh Feehan, a major figure on the London Irish scene throughout the 1950s and '60s. Tadgh had originally worked as a teacher in Yorkshire but left to become secretary of the Anti-Partition League, a post he held throughout the 1950s and early '60s. He was attached to the Irish Embassy and features in many of Paddy Fahey's photographs over four decades. Tadgh was also involved in county associations, the 1916 commemorations and numerous political and cultural groups. Front row, left to right: Tadgh Feehan, Ambassador Con Cremin, Tim Howard, Fr Hereton and Jim Conway.

The second photograph features Tadgh's retirement reception held at the Irish Embassy, 1984. Tadgh is being presented with a commemorative plaque by Paddy Hogan, the Chairman of the Federation of Irish Societies. The photograph also includes Seamus McGarry and Jerry Corr (third and fourth left). In many ways Paddy Fahey's and Tadgh's careers mirrored each other. Both were are at the heart of community politics throughout the entire period covered in this volume. It is perhaps fitting that this picture was one of the last recorded in Paddy's photographic diary.

Two other aspects of London Irish life. It is all too easy to think of the London Irish as builders and nurses and forget that the Irish Club in Eaton Square and the National University of Ireland Club at the Challoner Rooms often hosted events for a different class of Irish person. This photograph was taken in the early 1950s and features a group of unknown Irish medical golfers.

This image captures a National University of Ireland group on its way to a Buckingham Palace garden party, 1955. It includes, left to right: Michael McCormack (Tipperary), President of the National University Club, Mrs McCormack, Dr and Mrs Howlett (Wexford), Dr Tom Tangney (Cork) and Mrs Tangney.

Intellectual stimulation took many forms. The annual Terence MacSwiney lecture (pictured here in 1964) was a regular feature of the cultural scene in 1960s London. In the front row are Mr Ted McGrath and Mick Brown (first and second left) from Cork. In the third row is Maurice Sheehy (third from left) and in the second row is Winnie Anglin (second from left). Winnie was a member of Cuman Na mBan and fought in the GPO in the Revolution of 1916.

An Irish language class at Cricklewood Technical School, 1956. Standing on the extreme right is Tommy Murphy, the tutor. Did the women naturally congregate at the front of the class or was this language policy of the time?

The Hoxton Pioneer Total Abstinence Association Drama Group on stage, 1964. Amateur dramatics were very popular in Ireland in the 1950s and '60s, and the Pioneers were great champions of such activities as drama because they offered opportunities for social gatherings away from the pub.

A play being performed at the Sugawn Theatre, Hackney, c. 1974. The Sugawn probably wouldn't have gained the approval of the Pioneers since it was based in a pub.

Two photographs of the Sugawn Folk Kitchen in Hackney. The Sugawn was an important venue for the Irish cultural renaissance in 1960s and '70s London. Originally the Duke of Wellington pub, Jerry O'Neill took it over in the '60s and converted it into the Sugawn Folk Kitchen.

Throughout the 1970s, the Sugawn was the venue for many Irish cultural events. It staged numerous Irish plays and saw the finest of musicians perform. Paddy Fahey's studio was just around the corner in Dalston Lane, and as a result the Sugawn became a regular haunt for him over the years.

These Irish nurses from St Andrew's Hospital, Dollis Hill, were captured on film by Paddy Fahey when out carol singing in 1962.

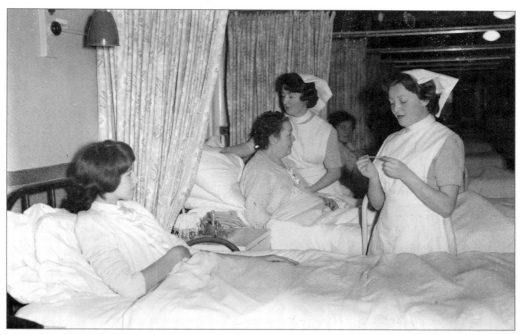

Although this is obviously a posed photograph, it still represents one of the only truly working photographs in Paddy's collection. Thousands of young Irish women trained as nurses in London hospitals throughout the 1950s and '60s. The NHS relied heavily on Irish and West Indian women to staff its hospitals throughout these years. Salaries for trainee nurses were small and it took a lot of dedication to stick with the work when higher wages were available for those who sought employment in industry.

A prize-giving ceremony at Whipps Cross Hospital, 1956. Most of the women in this photograph were Irish.

In the late 1950s, possibly 1957, Paddy Fahey took a series of photographs of young Irish women who were working at the Savoy Hotel in the Strand. This formal yet relaxed photograph records for posterity the Savoy's Irish chambermaids.

A fit of the giggles. These young nurses at St Andrew's just couldn't keep a straight face in this 1958 photograph.

Many among the established Irish community feared for the chances of the young Irish who arrived in the capital without contacts or much money. The Catholic clergy were particularly concerned to ensure that the young did not stray from the moral straight line. However, no funding was available publicly and all monies had to be raised from within the community. This photograph captures the committee of the Marion Women's Hostel at work in 1959. Those present include Charlie Butterfield, Fr McNamara, Paddy Watters and Marie Harrington.

Young women gather around the piano for a wholesome evening of singing at the Marion Women's Hostel, Hornsey Lane Gardens, Highgate. This is a heavily posed photograph.

Fr McNamara was the driving force behind many community movements. Here he is seen welcoming new arrivals to the hostel at the Irish Centre in Camden. Throughout the 1960s the Camden Irish Centre offered a vital service to the young immigrants, offering them advice, work contacts, a roof over their heads and a safe environment in which to socialize with other Irish people. Fr Mac subsequently became parish priest at St Gabriel's Church, which was located opposite the Gresham Ballroom. The establishment of the Centre in 1955 was very important for the development of the Irish community in London. It sponsored two hostels for young Irish people, the men's hostel (above) and the Marion Women's Hostel at Hornsey Lane Gardens. These initiatives were paid for by public subscription and many unpaid hours were given over to organizing fund-raisers, from bingo nights in church halls to grand concerts at the Albert Hall.

St Brendan's Hostel in Barnes, established with support from the Kerry Association in 1961. Inside, the Blessed Virgin Mary looks down on the proceedings. Cardinal Griffin, Archbishop of Westminster, wrote a pastoral letter in 1955 outlining a new approach for the care of immigrants. From this time the Church would attempt to materially assist the young immigrants: 'Given decent lodgings with a healthy Catholic atmosphere, contacts with his fellow Irishmen and a chance to secure a good job of work, there is no reason why he should not settle down happily, successfully and without danger to his faith.'

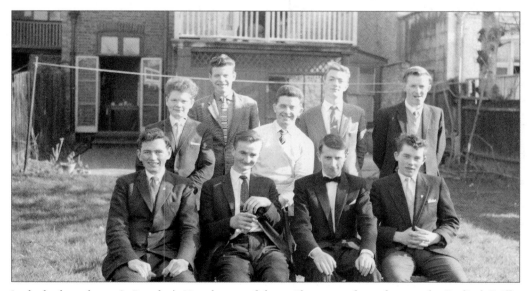

In the back garden at St Brendan's Hostel some of the residents pose for a photograph. Cardinal Griffin was particularly concerned about the age of the Irish immigrant: 'We have to face up to the fact that Catholic boys and girls, most of them in their teens, are crossing the Irish Sea in increasing numbers'. If this group is in any way representative then it is likely that children as young as fifteen and sixteen were emigrating during this period.

In contrast to the previous photographs, the Dublin Bachelors' Association, pictured here in the mid-1950s, were happy to fraternize with members of the opposite sex!

The Clare Association leads this 1958 St Patrick's Day Parade through Whitehall. In the middle is a banner from the Dublin Society; Dublin was not well represented among the London Irish of the 1950s. Throughout the years of greatest emigration the largest numbers of Irish emigrants always came from the south and west of the country.

SURELY A GAME

An action shot of the opening minutes of a London v Warwickshire Gaelic football match, 1951. The 1950s were glory years for the GAA in London. Given the huge amount of emigration to England in general and London in particular, most All-Ireland teams in the '50s were made up of significant numbers of London Irish.

There are records of Irish games being played in London since the eighteenth century. The Gaelic Athletic Association was established in the capital in 1895 and over the years some very famous Irishmen were associated with Irish sports. Perhaps the most infamous of all was the young Michael Collins who played for the Geraldines Club during his stay in London from 1906–15.

Throughout the twentieth century, the GAA has remained the most disciplined of London Irish organizations, and Gaelic games have never ceased to be played, even during the First and Second World Wars. The games were particularly strong in times of heavy emigration. From as early as the 1920s teams were regularly visiting from Ireland to play exhibition matches and to give a boost to the local game. But it was club football and hurling that were the backbone of Gaelic sporting life in London. Local clubs such as the Sean McDermotts, the Bros Pearse and the Brian Borus provided sporting outlets for players and spectators alike.

Other Gaelic sports such as camogie and handball were also played in London. Indeed even such sports as road bowling have been played with gusto on Sunday afternoons in Dagenham since the 1940s. Sport was more than a pastime – for many young emigrants it was a passport to a good job and a ready-made circle of friends within the community.

Undoubtedly the 1950s were the glory years for the GAA in London. Among the thousands of emigrants who arrived in London yearly were numerous hurling and football stars. Most All-Ireland teams of the period had players who lived in London. The attendances at sporting events were very large during those years. Thousands of Irish people crowded into Mitcham each year to see the matches played by the All-Ireland footballers and hurlers.

The photographs that follow capture some of the spirit of sporting life among Irish Londoners in the 1950s and '60s.

A group photograph taken during the Gaelic Athletic Association Convention held at St Anne's Football Club in the East End, 1958. The front row includes: Mick Walsh (president), Bill Cremin, Dan Murphy, Jack McCarthy, Johnnie Moriarty, Fr Tom McNamara (chairman), Jim Mullarkey (treasurer), John Dunne (secretary), Jerry Daly, Mick Parkinson, Bobby Baker, Paddy Donoghue.

Cumann Lúit Cleas Ʒaedeal —
c.c. Lonndain

(Gaelic Athletic Association—London County Board)

HURLING AND FOOTBALL Matches

EVERY SUNDAY AFTERNOON
Football 3.30, Hurling 4.45

at

G.A.A. SPORTS GROUNDS
Avery Hill Road, Eltham, S.E.9
Southern Railway from Charing Cross, Waterloo & London Bridge to New Eltham Station.

ST. COLMCILLE GROUNDS,
London Colony, St. Albans
(Adjoining London Colony Hospital)

DAGENHAM PARK,
Dagenham, Essex
(5 minutes walk from Princess Cinema)

ADDRESS YOUR ENQUIRIES TO CO. BOARD SECRETARY—
P. CASEY,
1 Monks Crescent, Walton-on-Thames, Surrey.

Woodgrange Press, Ltd., London, E.7.

After Mitcham, New Eltham was the most popular sports ground in the London area in the 1950s.

Tossing the coin at the beginning of the London v Warwickshire match. The match was played at Mitcham, the primary GAA venue at the time. Mitcham had been used by the GAA as its principal ground since 1938. The grounds had been built for Rugby League, but became the home of the GAA in London until the mid-1950s.

Tipperary hurlers in the foreground lead the walk on before their match against Wexford at Mitcham, 1954. In the 1920s the tradition had arisen of inviting the teams from the All-Ireland football and hurling finals to London for an exhibition match. The hurlers arrived for the Whitsun weekend and the footballers played their game at Easter. This practice continued until the games moved to Wembley in 1958. After that time both games were played at Whitsun.

Teams at London Airport, 1960. The arrival of the teams from Ireland created considerable difficulties for the local GAA organization. Indeed one of the ancillary reasons for the establishment of county associations was to help to provide accommodation and entertainment for the visiting teams.

A reception for the Dublin All-Ireland football team. Those present include Fr P. O'Toole (left), Chairman of the Dublin Society, and Eamonn Andrews, London's most famous Dubliner.

Hundreds of people crowded into Kensington Town Hall to see the MacCarthy Cup and the winning 1959 Waterford All-Ireland team. Pat Fanning is standing on the stage.

Hurling action at the London v Lancashire game, 1958.

The start of the Bros Pearse *v* Cuchullains game played at New Eltham, early 1950s. Bros Pearse was a very old club that began life in Peckham in 1920.

Whit Monday Programme.

St Monica's Gaelic Football Team before their match with St Patrick's, 1958. Standing on the extreme right is Michael Parkinson, a publican based in Fleet Street. Teams tended to change their bases over the years and were often focused on a particular pub or publican. When a well-known personality moved on from a pub he often took the football team with him.

Before the start of the London v Limerick junior match at New Eltham, early 1950s. Included in the picture are Jim Conway (back row, first left), Bill Brady (back row, third left), Blondy Murphy (back row, sixth right), John Dunne (back row, first right).

The GAA banner had pride of place in the 1965 St Patrick's Day parade. Here the marchers are seen turning into Parliament Square.

Sarsfields Camogie Team. This photograph was taken before their line out against Cuchullains in the South London Final at Wormwood Scrubs. Camogie was popular in the 1950s and teams regularly travelled to other parts of the country, for example Manchester and Warwickshire, to play matches.

Irish wrestlers at the Galtymore Club, Cricklewood, 1958. Wrestling was a popular sport among the Irish. The most famous of all wrestling stars of the era was the Ballydehob man, Dan O'Mahony, who was famous for his Irish Whip.

This great action shot truly captures the excitement of an athletics meeting with this tug-o-war team taking the strain. Many of these men would be footballers participating in tug-o-war to keep fit.

The long jump. This sports meeting was held between London and Louth NACA. The venue was probably Blackheath in South London. Although the year of the meeting is uncertain, it is unlikely to be later than 1958.

There was a large turn-out for the 1961 annual general meeting of the Brian Borus Gaelic Football Club. The Brian Borus was the oldest club in London, having been founded in 1900.

Sean McDermotts' annual general meeting, 1957. This is a very evocative photograph: one can almost smell the stale cigarette smoke today. Those present include Fr McNamara (third right), Jim Mullahy, the founder of the Sean McDermotts (fourth right). Facing the camera in the centre is Timmy Sheehan, who later played for the Brian Borus.

A view of the stand before the start of the Kerry *v* Dublin match held at Mitcham, mid-1950s. The Mitcham grounds were offered to the GAA for purchase at about this time, but they were unable to raise the asking price. The result was that the best venue that Irish London possessed passed out of its hands and was eventually redeveloped as part of a housing scheme.

An evocative view of the terraces. This may have been taken at Woolwich in the mid-1950s in the years before the games moved to Wembley.

The GAA march in the 1962 St Patrick's Day parade through Whitehall with a banner advertising the Whitsun Games at Wembley. Irish people came from all over Britain to London at Whitsun.

The unveiling of a memorial to Sean Og Hanley at Kensal Rise Cemetery, mid-1950s. Sean Og Hanley was a member of the first Limerick hurling team to win the All-Ireland of 1897. He lived and died in London. Kneeling in the centre with his back to the camera is Fr McNamara, a stalwart of all such events.

ON BENDED KNEE

Blessing of religious objects at the women's mission at the Church of Notre Dame, Camden. The missions were held regularly in Catholic churches in Ireland and England throughout this period. For two weeks and sometimes longer missionary priests, the stormtroopers of the Church, descended on a parish and harangued the faithful with talk of sin and hell. Separate missions were held for women and men because of the large numbers of the faithful who attended the missions.

The majority of Irish Londoners in the 1950s and '60s were members of the Catholic faith. Church attendances were very large and the Church was devotional in character. Sodalities, missions, devotions and fraternities were very well attended by the London Irish Catholics.

But the Church also played a much wider role in everyday life. Catholic nuns educated the young children of the immigrants, Irish nurses often trained in Catholic hospitals. The clergy, because of their standing within the community, turn up in all of Paddy Fahey's photographs. Whether the event is a county association meeting or a sports event, a seaside trip or a children's party, there was normally a member of the clergy on hand to oversee events. The priest was a natural leader for the community.

The Catholic Church in London owed a great debt to the Irish community. Irish Catholics had formed the backbone of much of the London Church since Victorian times. However, it wasn't until Cardinal Griffin's pastoral letter of 1955 that the plight of Irish immigrants was officially considered by the Church. From the 1950s right through to the '70s the devotionalist nature of Irish Catholicism meant that a great strain was put on the diocese of Westminister. Churches were filled to overflowing in Irish areas, the most spectacular of all being Quex Road, Kilburn, where some twenty-one masses were celebrated each Sunday. It was fortunate that this period coincided with the peak in vocations to the Catholic priesthood in Ireland. Thus there were plenty of Irish priests available to serve in London parishes and to see to the spiritual needs of their countrypeople.

The bended knee of the London Irish can easily be misunderstood in the changed climate of the present day. The Irish Catholic Church was not imposed from above but grew organically from the people. While the Church of the day was often overbearing and punitive, it was – especially in the immigrant context – also an institution that genuinely cared for the well-being, both spiritual and physical, of its members. This fact was well known to the people captured on film by Paddy Fahey in the following pages.

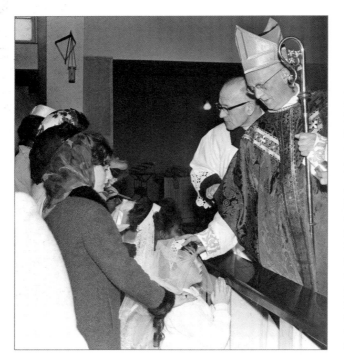

A belt of the Crosier! This 1967 confirmation ceremony at St John the Baptist's Church, Tottenham, was conducted by Cardinal Heenan. Archbishop Heenan succeeded Archbishop Godfrey in the See of Westminister in 1963 and was elevated to Cardinal in 1965. Both black and white children were coming to church in the increasingly multicultural environment of London. From this period right up to the 1980s some Catholic parishes experienced tension between Irish parishioners who had established themselves in the 1950s and new Commonwealth arrivals from the Catholic West Indian islands such as St Lucia.

Looking after the Catholic Truth Society bookstall. The Catholic Truth Society was originally founded in 1868 by Cardinal Vaughan while still a diocesan priest. In 1964 it received an honour from Pope Paul VI, 'Publisher to the Holy See'. This photograph is taken outside their main office in Westminster.

The renewal of baptismal vows at the close of the men's mission at the Church of the Sacred Heart, Quex Road, Kilburn. Church attendance in the 1950s and '60s was probably as high among Irish Londoners as it was among the native population in Ireland, with young men and women thronging to church in large numbers. The effect was so great that the population of the diocese of Westminister increased by over 30 per cent in the decade after the Second World War. In Quex Road during the heyday of church attendance from the 1950s to '70s Sunday mass attendance was in the region of 14,000. The numbers were so great that loudspeakers were wired up in the yard so that mass could be broadcast to the huge overspill of parishioners outside. Even the neighbouring Methodist church was used as an additional venue for masses.

This charming photograph is possibly of Fr Eoin Sweeney, a popular priest among the London Irish, and an unknown child in the newly dedicated John F. Kennedy Memorial Hall at the Camden Irish Centre.

Keegan-Doyle wedding in Clerkenwell, 1959. The wedding party stands outside the Church of St Peter and St Paul, Amwell Street. This was a parish that was evenly matched with Irish and Italian parishioners. The priest on the left may be Fr Ginty of Quex Road.

Cutting the cake at the O'Regan wedding, mid-1950s. Although Paddy Fahey worked as a press photographer throughout the 1950s and '60s, he also ran a very successful studio. Weddings were a staple part of his business throughout and they helped to make him known to the Irish community at large. Paddy's photographic diaries record hundreds of weddings, but sadly very few of these photographs survive.

Opposite. On bended knee. A kiss for Cardinal Brown's ring from a member of the faithful, Theresa Walsh, at a reception held in his honour at the Irish Club, Eaton Square. Theresa was the Secretary of the Tipperary Association, which hosted the event. Cardinal Brown was originally from Tipperary and was, when this photograph was taken in 1962, a very successful career cleric who held a position in the Curia in Rome.

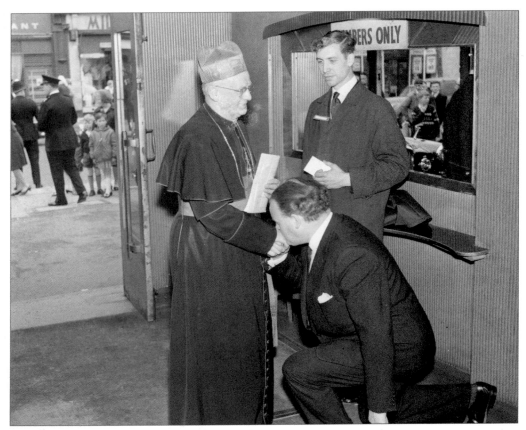

The sacred and the profane. This photograph was taken during a Legion of Mary mass at the Galtymore Club. Cardinal Heenan officiated at the mass. In the background is the Cricklewood Broadway. After the mass it is likely that the Legion staged a dance, a fairly regular practice at the time.

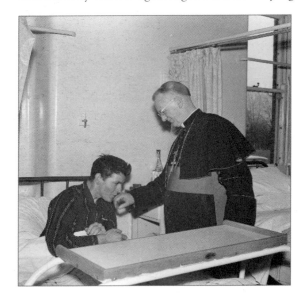

The corporal works of mercy. Here Paddy captures a visit by Archbishop Heenan to St Andrew's Hospital, Dollis Hill, in 1964. There was always a high proportion of Irish nurses working at St Andrew's.

In 1951 St Patrick's seminary in Thurles hosted a reunion for its past pupils. This was the era of large numbers of vocations to the Catholic Church in Ireland. Ireland was producing so many priests in those years that they were able to export hundreds all over the world. Many went on missions to the developing world and many came to England to serve in the industrial cities where large numbers of young Irish lived.

Archbishop Godfrey with members of the Oblate community at the Church of the Sacred Heart, Quex Road, Kilburn, 1958. Front row, left to right: Fr Purcell (parish priest), Archbishop Godfrey, Fr Toland, Fr Ginty; back row: Fr O'Donovan (parish priest of Percy Road church, which was officially part of Quex Road at the time), Fr O'Toole, Fr Wall, Fr Callaly. The photograph was probably taken after a confirmation ceremony. The priests at Quex Road played a significant role in local Irish life, organizing events in the church hall and seeing to the social needs of their parishioners.

Next to churches the other large institutions available to the London Irish were the dancehalls. This image
and the following one record two services at two of London's most famous dancehalls. In the top
photograph is a section of the faithful who packed the Galtymore Ballroom in Cricklewood for a Legion of
Mary service in 1967. The Legion, founded in Dublin in 1921, did a lot of charitable work helping the
more deprived members of the community.

The Augustinian priests who ran the parish church in Hammersmith knew that it was too small to house
the numbers expected to attend the mission in 1973. As a result the neighbouring Irish dancehall, the
Hibernian Club, was pressed into service for the duration of the mission. The ballroom was changed little
in order to accommodate the faithful. The board to the left of the stage displays a sign advertising Margo
and The Country Folk.

Interior of St Mary's and St Andrew's Church, Dollis Hill Lane, Willesden, 1966. A special mass is being celebrated for the Pioneer Total Abstinence Association. This photograph was taken at the end of mass when the Deacon sang, 'Ite, Missa Est', and the congregation replied, 'Deo Gratias'. Today the priest would say in the vernacular, 'The mass is ended'.

Church and State. Eamon De Valera was Taoiseach in the late 1950s when this photograph was taken at a National University of Ireland St Patrick's Day reception. He is deep in conversation with Archbishop Godfrey of Westminster, one of the pre-eminent clerics in Britain.

This whimsical picture was taken by Paddy at St
Andrew's Convent, Dollis Hill, Willesden,
during their jubilee celebrations in 1963. St
Andrew's had been built before the First World
War and staffed by the Poor Servants of the
Mother of God. Initially it was intended to
house, among others, French-speaking patients.
Its Catholic ethos and its position in the heavily
Irish populated Borough of Willesden inevitably
meant that by the postwar years there would be a
large Irish influence in the hospital.

The Irish Sisters of Charity were invited to take
over the running of a residential school on
Sternhall Street, Walthamstow, from the Sisters
of Mercy in 1929. Their convent, St Mary's, was
associated with Our Lady and St George's
Church. This photograph was taken by Paddy
Fahey in 1958 when the nuns were celebrating
the centenary of the convent school.

Both the photographs on this page feature the work of the Pioneer Total Abstinence Association. Here a group resplendent with their Pioneer pins pose after a Pioneer rally. It might have been taken after a novena at Highgate Church.

Members of the Dollis Hill Pioneer Council pose outside St Mary's and St Andrew's Church, Dollis Hill, Willesden, 1966. Contrary to stereotypical views temperance had a long history in Ireland, going back to the huge temperance rallies of Fr Matthew in the middle of the nineteenth century. Many young emigrants to London had taken the pledge at the time of their confirmation and many kept temperate for the rest of their lives. Front row, left to right: Pat O'Toole, J. McGettigan, Ann Maher, Fr Jones (parish priest), T. Mullally, P. St George; back row: Pat Ryan, Alice Dwane, Paddy O'Connor, B. O'Connor, Martin Ryan.

A large gathering outside the Catholic Truth Society shop at 28a Ashley Place, Westminster, 1958. The priest is Fr O'Toole of the Quex Road church, so it is likely that some of the crowd are from among his parishioners. Fr O'Toole was well known for his fine singing voice.

The crowds were so great at the arrival of Archbishop Dalton, Cardinal of Armagh, in London that many were forced to remain outside the Archbishop Amigo Jubilee Hall at St George's RC Cathedral, Southwark, in 1954.

Fr Eamonn Casey dominates this picture taken at the Galwaymen's Association dinner at the Camden Irish Centre, 1969. In the 1960s Fr Casey was a well-known cleric in London, where he did a lot of work on housing issues and the Irish community. He subsequently returned to Ireland and became Bishop of Kerry and later Bishop of Galway. In 1992 he resigned his bishopric having admitted to fathering a son. By the late 1990s he was living and working as a priest in Mexico.

Tipperary women welcome the Archbishop of Cashel. The wording of their ever so humble address to the Archbishop deserves transcribing in full since it encapsulates so much about the relationship of priest and people at the time, both in Ireland and among the London Irish: 'To the most Reverend Dr Thomas Morris, Archbishop of Cashel and Emly. On the occasion of this your first visit to The Tipperary Men's Association of London, the executive committee and the members of the Association tender to your Grace their respectful greetings and their deep gratitude for your gracious acceptance of the office of Patron of the Association. We feel highly honoured that so distinguished a son of Tipperary should find the time and make the opportunity to visit those of his spiritual sons and daughters now in London. We are aware of the great work you have done for our people in Muintir Na Tire. We know something of your reputation as a scholar. We know much of your pastoral good, both as priest and now as Archbishop. We promise to remember both you and your great Archdiocese in our prayers and we ask, respectfully, that sometimes you will remember before the altar, your scattered children in London, that they may at all times be faithful to God, to the Holy Church and to Tipperary.'

Theresa Walsh, Secretary of the Tipperary Men's Association, is on the left.

SUFFER LITTLE CHILDREN

*A little girl from the Agnes O'Connell Band, 1957.
Children were enrolled in dancing classes from the age of
four onwards.*

For the majority of London Irish children life was dominated by Irish themes. Early schooling was usually conducted by the nuns, and religious festivals marked the school year. Extra-curricular activities for many (girls in particular) included the Saturday morning Irish dancing class with regular participation in dance and music competitions. Holidays normally entailed going 'home' to Ireland for three weeks in August, usually to stay with Irish relatives. While in Ireland, their Irish cousins and neighbours saw them as English and parodied their English accents.

Sadly many of this generation came of age in the 1970s at a time of popular anti-Irish feeling in Britain. Ironically, attempts by some to assert their Irishness in the face of tabloid racism was sometimes dismissed by first-generation Irish people with the derogatory epithet 'Plastic Paddy'. For some the legacy of their upbringing was an inability to fit into either British or Irish culture. On a more positive note, however, second-generation Irish Londoners are now closely associated with the renaissance of Irish popular culture, Irish studies and the arts. Many have now gone on to raise a third generation of Irish Londoners who are still aware and proud of their Irish roots. For the people who experienced this reality the following pages will evoke something of a London Irish childhood.

First Holy Communicants at Quex Road church flanked by two nuns. The convent was based at Compayne Gardens, West Hampstead. First Communicants were always told that this was the greatest day of their lives.

Children stepdancing at an athletics meeting at Mitcham, 1951. They are wearing their hornpipe shoes, made of black patent leather with silver buckles.

Plucked from the chorus line at a feis, an Irish festival, 1952. The standard uniform consisted of green pleated skirt, white blouse, bolero, a little shawl and occasionally a tarn brooch.

Interior of a classroom at the Sisters of Mercy School at Kensal New Town, Kensal Rise, 1965. Bambi, Holy Mary and the continual presence of a heavily garbed nun will evoke early memories of school for many second-generation Irish Londoners.

Opposite. The crowning of the Blessed Virgin Mary was the climax of an annual procession organized by the Sisters of Mercy at Kensal New Town. For the child chosen to perform the ceremony there was the glory of being centre stage. For the little girls who assisted, seen here, there was less glamour. The 1950s was a decade of great Marian devotion which had its peak in the celebrations of the Marian Year of 1954.

A children's party probably organized by the Wexford Association. There was little reason for these children to doubt their cultural roots. Many would have been regular attenders at Saturday Irish dancing classes. When it came to party entertainment the Wexford Association provided traditional music in the shape of the fiddler in the background.

The feast after the First Holy Communion ceremony at Marylebone, 1960.

Children at the Forresters' dance at Battersea, 1965. This scene is included here because it recalls memories of children at adult events – new clothes, long nights and bottles of crush.

The momentous events of the Easter Rising whose fiftieth anniversary celebrations were held at the Royal Albert Hall were probably lost on these children who performed at the event. No doubt they would best remember the white-bread sandwiches and the bottles of pop.

Stepping it out at the Feis Breiffne, 1970. This wonderful action shot captures the excitement of the dance competitions that were so much a part of young Irish Londoners' lives. The dancers are wearing soft shoes and the costumes have become more ornate than those common in the 1950s.

Crowning of the Blessed Virgin Mary, 1959. This was the climax of the annual procession organized by the Mercy nuns at the Church of Our Lady, Bosworth Road, Kensal New Town, Kensal Rise. Paddy Fahey made many trips to Kensal over the years to photograph events at the behest of the nuns. Crownings stopped in the 1970s, probably as a result of Vatican II's move away from devotionalism to a more cerebral faith.

BALLROOMS OF ROMANCE

*Big Tom at the Galtymore Club, Cricklewood, 1969. 'Send them home sweating' was the motto of the bands.
But it wasn't just the audience who left the dancehall with shirts clinging to their backs. Big Tom was well
known for giving good value for his entrance fee. And when the show was over the star still had to sign
hundreds of autographs.*

The ballroom was integral to London Irish life. With a vibrant history which ran back to before the Second World War, Irish ballrooms were a unique achievement of the time. The ballrooms that are recorded by Paddy Fahey were at their peak during the 1950s and '60s. All over London Irish people regularly crowded into ballrooms to dance to the Irish music stars of the day. Numerous such glamorous institutions existed in the capital: the Galtymore, the Banba, the Blarney Stone, the Shamrock, the Gresham, the Buffalo, the New Emerald and many more smaller halls. They served the needs of a huge Irish population starved of contact with home. Like all aspects of Irish life, London ballrooms were complex institutions. They were usually owned by Irish entrepreneurs, men such as Mick Gannon, who were prominent in Irish life in the capital.

The photographs captured by Paddy Fahey in the ballrooms of romance are special. They do not record the images of important people in the community – there are no presidents or chairmen of community associations, no religious dignitaries, no politicians. Instead these photographs show a simple cross-section of ordinary London Irish life as it enjoyed itself at the weekend.

A section of the vast crowd which packed into the Galtymore Club in Cricklewood to see the first great Irish superstar, Bridie Gallagher. Bridie forged a new path singing Irish ballads to a crossover audience in Britain. She appeared on the BBC's *Sunday Night at the Palladium* and subsequently on the *Ed Sullivan Show* in the United States.

The resident band at the Galtymore Club, Cricklewood, 1961. Front row, left to right: Gabriel O'Sculley, Jack Coughlan (both from Galway), Kit O'Connor, Michael McMahon (from Clare); back row: Danny Ahern (the MC from Cork), Frank Mahony (from Clare).

This is an unusual photograph from the Galty as the band on stage is not the resident band. According to Danny Ahern, this band was a stand-in put together after a last-minute cancellation. The only resident band member was Kit O'Connor, the accordionist. This band, and the one in the top photograph, were residents in the céilí hall. The Galty catered for all Irish tastes with a céilí area and a modern area. The modern side also had a regular band and both areas featured guest bands, which included some of the biggest stars of the day.

A trip out of London, this time for a céilí at Maidstone in Kent, *c.* 1959. The happy participants are probably dancing to Paul Jones and are wearing Pioneer pins, floral-print dresses and Sunday suits.

No jiving allowed. Many of the Irish dancehalls in the 1950s displayed signs banning jiving and for the hardy individuals who flouted the rules there was a firm tap on the shoulder from the MC. Things were a little more relaxed at the Waterfordmen's Association dinner dance in the mid-1950s, seen here – an early example of jiving occurring in close proximity to the more traditional quickstep!

A fresh-faced Brendan Bowyer and the Royal showband backstage with admirers at the Galtymore Club, Cricklewood, 1966. Brendan Bowyer's 'Hucklebuck' was one of the biggest showband hits of the 1960s. Note the embossed images of Ireland on the wallpaper.

On stage at the Galtymore, Brendan is subject to adulation from the crowd. These sessions allowed little room for dancing as it was standing room only. This show was in the modern section of the Galty.

A million miles away from the sharp-suited showbands of the 1960s were the ceilidhs and the set dancing of the previous generation. Here dancers are stopping the show at the Armagh Men's Association dance in about 1951. They are probably dancing the Duke Ri, a three-couple dance from Ulster popular at the time.

Galway Junior Association dance. By 1966 the fashions had changed and it is obvious that these young people, some first-generation born, some recent immigrants, have borrowed a lot from the dominant youth culture of the Beatles era.

The Rainbow Club changed its name several times. It was best known as the Slievenamon. Its proprietor in the 1960s was Maurice Lane.

Dr Bill Loughnane and the Tulla Ceilidh Band on stage at the Shamrock Rooms at the Elephant and Castle, a major venue for young Irish from all around South London at the time. The Elephant was situated at a major bus and tube junction and so was accessible by public transport from most parts of London.

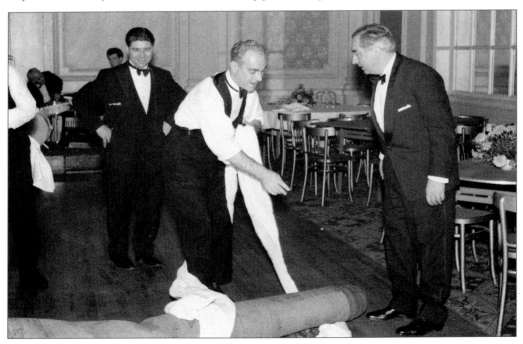

Joe Lynch at the Banba Club, Kilburn, 1955. Joe was a popular Radio Eireann broadcaster and could draw immense crowds on his trips to London. The Banba was owned by Mike Gannon, a Sligo man, who also owned the Blarney Stone in Tottenham Court Road.

Opposite. Rolling up the carpet after the meal in preparation for the dance at the annual Cork Association dinner, 1966. The man supervising the operation on the right is none other than George Brown, later Lord Brown. Brown was the notoriously difficult Foreign Secretary in Harold Wilson's Labour government. He was also Cork born, hence his presence at the dinner.

Val Doonican at the Innisfree Club, 1965. Val originally came from Waterford and emigrated to London in the early 1950s. In 1965 he was finally discovered and was given his own Saturday-night programme by the BBC. The runaway success of his TV shows meant that he was one of the most famous Irishmen in England when this photograph was taken.

Bridie Gallagher receives a bouquet of flowers from an admirer at the Galtymore Club in Cricklewood. At the height of her fame Bridie was reported to command a fee of £100 per appearance. At the Galty she would come on stage for only a short set of five or six songs.

The famous Dublin priest Fr Michael Cleary on stage at the Galtymore Club, 1965. Fr Cleary, who was known as 'The Singing Priest', had his own cabaret act which he toured with in Ireland and Britain. He was very popular with Irish people in London and at home throughout the 1960s, '70s and '80s. He introduced the Pope to the Galway youth mass of 1979 and died in Dublin in 1993. After his death a major controversy resulted from the discovery of his secret family, a female partner and a son.

Fr Cleary on stage at an unknown venue in London. This image is on a roll of film that Paddy Fahey shot in the days running up to the Easter Rising jubilee celebrations of 1966. It is not clear whether the dance was in any way connected with that event.

By 1972 Brendan Bowyer was fronting the Big 8 showband with Twink as the leading female vocalist. Second from the left is Paddy Cole. The Big 8 subsequently moved to Las Vegas where they continued to perform in cabaret up to the 1980s. This probably mirrors the changing fortunes of the band scene. By the mid-1970s the heyday of the ballroom era in Ireland was over, the emergence of discos and nightclubs with their drink licences and changing patterns of leisure made it far more difficult for the majority of dancehalls to continue. Paradoxically it would appear that ballrooms continued to flourish in London after they had begun to wane in popularity in Ireland.

Handbill advertising events for St Patrick's Night at the Shamrock Club, Elephant and Castle, 1955.

The Banba was one of the most famous of all Irish dancehalls. It featured dances all week and tea dances on Sundays. The Banba also broadcast GAA matches from Ireland. A woman who danced at the Banba in the 1960s recalled that the dance floor would clear for the duration of the match and that the men would return with enthusiasm after five o'clock.

For those of us who went to dances in the 1970s the photographs on this page will bring back memories of flares, queues, the cold, the rain, and working up a sweat in your crimplene dress or cheesecloth shirt. This is the queue outside the Hibernian Club on the Fulham Broadway.

On stage is Joe Mac, lead singer with Stage 2. Mac was a zany performer who originally came from Cork. By the late 1970s and early '80s he was concentrating on business, as he ran a very successful restaurant in the Queen's Old Castle in Cork.

The photographs on this page capture the excitement surrounding the first performance by Big Tom at the Galty. Big Tom became known as the king of country and Irish music. Country and Irish was very popular among the London Irish from the late 1960s onwards. Although easily lampooned as sentimental nonsense, the words of the popular ballads often struck a chord with lonely immigrants. 'Shall I ne'er see you more, Gentle Mother?' were the opening lines from Big Tom's famous hit 'Gentle Mother'. For many young people in London, living away from home for the first time, these lines went deep to their own hearts. Big Tom was no stranger to London, having lived there in the early 1960s. Dancehalls did not sell alcohol so a bottle of 7 Up was all that a star could drink when meeting his fans.

On stage with the Mainliners. When Tom wasn't singing lead he took a back seat by playing saxophone in the band. He rarely went off stage after his own set.

The twisting sisters. Here two nurses do the twist at a benefit dance for SS John and Elizabeth Hospice. The benefit was organized by Mrs Boland, the wife of the Irish Ambassador.

A tour by Wexford Mummers to London in 1961 included a performance at the Gresham on the Holloway Road. The mummers' dance is peculiar to County Wexford, where legend has it that the dance was adapted from the dance of French sailors saved from shipwreck. Included in the photograph are Leo Carty (first left), Tommy Moloney, Pat O'Brien, Jackie Grindon (sixth–eighth left), Ted Kelly (second from right).

The Agnes O'Connell Band in full flight, 1960. Agnes is leading, front left. On St Patrick's Day the Agnes O'Connell Band travelled to a number of the major dancehalls, arriving mid-performance, doing a quick circuit of the hall and playing a few sets. A story was told to me about a St Patrick's Night at the Galtymore when a hapless Galwayman failed to get out of the way of Agnes' swinging baton and ended the night with a very sore head.

A handbill advertising an appearance by Delia Murphy in the 1950s. Delia was born in Mayo and was most famous for her two songs 'If I were a Blackbird' and 'The Spinning Wheel', both of which were played every St Patrick's Day as the BBC's main contribution to the Irish national holiday throughout the late 1950s.

Derry-born Josef Locke was always sure to pack out the Galtymore. This appearance was in the mid-1950s. Joe, born Joseph McLaughlin, became a great hit in Britain in the late 1940s and '50s. He is famous for his legendary nineteen summer seasons at Blackpool.

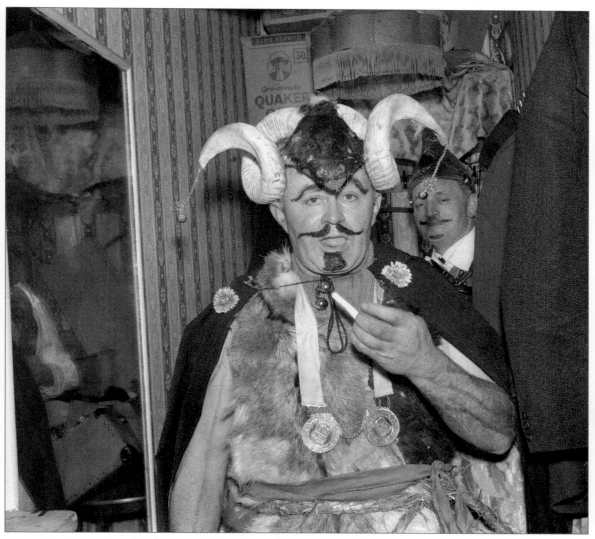

The Wren King did the rounds of Irish London in 1964 and visited Holloway, Cricklewood and Hammersmith, where Paddy Fahey took this photograph. In the early years of the twentieth century Wren dances were big affairs throughout much of rural Ireland. Now the tradition of Wren boys is largely relegated to a children's trick-or-treat style performance. The Wren dance features heavily in the book *The Bodhran Makers* by J.B. Keane, a man who lived in London as an immigrant and has written very eloquently about the life of the London Irish.

An interior view of the Blarney Club in Tottenham Court Road. The Blarney and the Banba were both owned by Mick Gannon, who like all proprietors booked bands to perform across both venues. From the early 1950s famous artists like Martin Crosbie, Delia Murphy and Billy Carter all performed at the Blarney.

Paddy took this photograph while covering a function at the Four Provinces Gaelic Football Club, 1956. The club used to meet at the Red Lion in Kilburn in those years but it is not known for certain if this photograph was taken there. Perhaps somebody who drank there will get in contact to let us know?

Interior view of the Blarney Club, 31 Tottenham Court Road. The sign on the wall advertises flights to Ireland, but very few Irish Londoners could afford regular trips by plane. For the vast majority travel to and from home entailed a full day's journey by train and boat.

THE BLARNEY CLUB

This Card will admit you on any Tuesday, Thursday, Friday, Saturday, Sunday afternoon or evening.

31 Tottenham Court Road

Complimentary ticket to the Blarney Club, Tottenham Court Road.

Sugawn Kitchen, Hackney, 1969. John and Joan Clifford from Tralee were regulars at the Sugawn. John is seated with the accordion.

In 1960 Maurice Mulcahy and his orchestra played the Galtymore. Here, an enthusiastic couple dance to the big band sound. Meanwhile, below, the brass section go through their paces.

An appreciative crowd watches as two young women entertain this Donegal social, 1959. Generally speaking the west of Ireland men had little time for what was called modern dancing, and woe betide the dancehall manager who misjudged his audience. The device adopted by the more canny proprietors such as the Byrne brothers, who owned a string of dancehalls throughout Britain, was to split your audience, allowing the traditionalists to dance on one floor while making another floor available for those with more modern tastes. These women are probably dancing a two-hand reel.

Dancing a hornpipe at the beginning of the West London Irish Society social, 1970.

The ballad boom of the 1960s was a natural progression from the céilí orchestras of the '40s and '50s. A band of fine musicians cut their teeth on the ceilidh music scene. The musicians recorded at this unknown event in 1965 include, left to right: Liam Farrell, Raymond Roland, -?-, Kevin Taylor. Liam Farrell and Raymond Roland played together for many years at the White Hart on the Fulham Broadway, a very well-known traditional music venue.

A ballad competition at the Gresham on the Holloway Road, 1966. The traditional instruments have disappeared and the young hopefuls follow the example of the Clancy Brothers and the Dubliners, relying on several strong singers to belt out a tune. Guitars are also now becoming dominant.

The Melody Aces line up outside their van, 1962. In the early days the majority of Irish bands toured England during Lent, a time of no dances in Ireland (with the exception of St Patrick's Day). The Melody Aces were based in Newtownstewart, County Tyrone, and played very much in the big band tradition, featuring a large brass section. Those present include, left to right: John Devine, David Cole, -?-, Eugene McNamee, Jim Henderson, Patsey McGonagle, -?-, -?-.

The Fontana showband, 1968. This band played a very different style of music to the Melody Aces but the gruelling life on the road was no different.

Eamonn Andrews was a suave performer who knew well how to work an audience. That, together with his standing as a well-known Irishman in Britain, made him an ideal choice to act as master of ceremonies for the first Rose of Tralee competition in London. Here he is on his way up to the stage in 1959.

A highly posed shot of Aer Lingus beauty
contestants, 1959. In the days before women's
liberation a job as an Aer Lingus stewardess was
considered the ultimate in glamour among
Irishwomen.

Noel Purcell plants a kiss on the cheek of a contestant in the London heats of the Rose of Tralee
competition, 1960. First on the left is Eileen Scally, a young London Irishwoman who won the title
'London Rose'. Eileen was a past pupil of St Aloysius's Convent, Euston.

By the 1970s the days of the beauty contest were numbered. For this unknown participant in the Holiday Queen Competition, however, the lure of a free week at the Festival of Kerry made it all worthwhile. This photograph was probably taken at the Galtymore Club, Cricklewood.

Worries over the objectification of women obviously did not concern the organizers of this 1962 Miss Limerick competition. The late 1950s and '60s were the era of beauty contests and the London Irish participated enthusiastically in the phenomenon. What was going through the heads of the women behind the numbers 1–8 we shall never know.

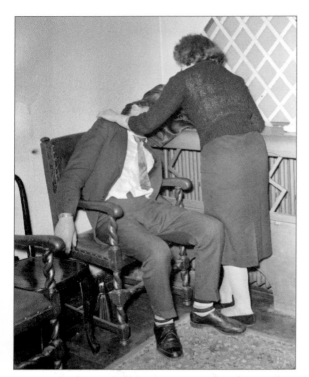 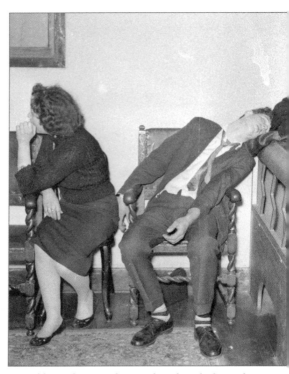

This set of images is unique in Paddy Fahey's collection. As a jobbing photographer working largely for Irish newspapers, Paddy had little encouragement to document Irish life beyond political, religious, sporting or leisure events. This study of a couple at a ceilidh in Maidstone in Kent in 1959 is the only such image in his collection. The deftness of touch makes one wish that Paddy had engaged in more social documentary.

FOUR GREEN FIELDS

The 1966 jubilee celebrations commemorating the fiftieth anniversary of the 1916 Rising were occasions of self-conscious pride and swagger for the Irish state. In London there were elaborate celebrations culminating in a major rally in Trafalgar Square. Here the Old IRA, the people who took particular pride of place in the proceedings, march along Whitehall.

On first looking at the Fahey photographs that relate to Irish political events one is struck by the strangeness of the images. Here are self-confident images of old gunmen parading their flags through Whitehall, in the heart of the empire against which they spent their youth fighting.

Paddy Fahey's political photographs of the Old IRA are truely historic. He was able to record for posterity the images of a generation that had fought to establish the Irish state. By the 1960s these men and women were old and most would soon die. Their position of respect in the community mirrored the situation in Ireland where the generation of men who were still leading the country in the 1950s were all ex-gunmen.

The intricacies of Irish government policies towards Northern Ireland and Britain are all played out through Paddy's photographs, in particular the mass support for the work of the Anti-Partition League. The visiting dignitaries were all in London primarily to affect British policy towards Ireland, not to minister to the needs of the Irish emigrant.

The irony of this must not have been lost on many Irish Londoners. Emigration had become endemic in Irish society. In the 1950s emigration figures from the Republic were as high as 400,0000, or some 14 per cent of its population. Most Irish emigrants to London were there because the Irish state was unable to provide for its own citizens. The ambiguities of Irish politicians' attitudes towards the London Irish is clear in the following photographs. Politicians attended the set piece events such as dinner dances and spoke hopeful words about Ireland's future. Yet Irish economic plans throughout the period tacitly accepted that emigration would remain a way of life for a large section of the Irish population.

Ambassador Boland features in many of the photographs. He was a pivotal figure in the development of the Irish community in London during these years. Paddy Fahey credited him with the establishment of a proper concern for ordinary Irish immigrants at diplomatic level. Boland had a brilliant career in the Irish Diplomatic Service. He had served under Sean MacBride in Dublin as Secretary of the Department of External Affairs in the late 1940s. In 1950 he was appointed to London and took an active role in Irish life during his tenure in Britain. Boland appears to have recognized the importance of Paddy Fahey's work and always made him welcome at Embassy events. In retrospect we can see that such ease of access led to some very important political events being recorded for posterity.

This is an historic early photograph of the Trooping of the Colour in Parliament Square, 1951. Anecdotal evidence suggests that 25–30,000 people regularly attended these celebrations.

Captain Murphy of the Old IRA leads the St Patrick's Day parade past Big Ben, 1963. Jack Dempsey, a former member of the West Cork Brigade, Old IRA, is the flagbearer. Jack survived a severe rifle-butt attack in his youth and was reputed to have borne the scars for the rest of his life.

The St Patrick's Day parade was an opportunity for all of the London Irish to get out and flaunt their nationality at a time when many advertisements for accommodation still stipulated no Irish or coloured. Political groups like Cumann na h-Eireann Aontuighte were able to parade their aims for a united Ireland openly in Whitehall. The United Ireland Association, as it was known in English, replaced the Anti-Partition League. This photograph was taken in 1963 or '64. The banners, the lapel badges and the accompanying pipers were all part of life for the children of the first-generation immigrants.

The annual Terence McSwiney march from Brixton to St George's Cathedral, Southwark, mid-1950s. This was represented as an important platform for Irish politicians establishing their republican credentials. A youthful Jack Lynch, recently retired All-Ireland hurler, sitting TD (Member of the Irish parliament) and all-round Corkman, was proud to march behind the Anti-Partition League banner here.

Members of the Michael Collins Society pose for a photograph, 1963. The society campaigned for, among other things, the erection of blue plaques on houses associated with the young Collins, who lived in London between 1906 and 1915. Included in the photograph are, front row, left to right: Michael Quinn, Kevin Smith, Paudy Lynch and Finbarr Lehane. Paudy Lynch spent a lifetime in London associated with political campaigns concerning Irish issues, including Old IRA, immigrant welfare, police relations and the promotion of Irish trade.

This evocative photograph captures a night-time march, possibly in Camden Town. The march is an IRA fundraiser and it is led by a very familiar figure on the Irish scene, the 6 ft Sligo man, Larry O'Dowd. In the foreground, right, is Frank Lee, a prominent member of the Old IRA who was most famous among the London Irish for his Tara Ceilidh band that played all the major dance venues in the capital in the 1940s and '50s.

The 1916 Rising was the act that set in train the establishment of the Irish state. The generation of Irish people who were living in London in the 1960s were truly the sons and daughters of that revolution. The 1966 jubilee celebrations unleashed a huge outpouring of popular sentiment in Ireland. The year was marked by commemorations, publications, exhibitions and the launch of the epic film *Mise Eire*. In London a similar explosion of feeling occurred. The culmination of the event was the rally in Trafalgar Square. The Old IRA led the commemorations. By the mid-1960s these men and women were elderly and this was their moment of crowning glory. The Abbey actor Eddie Golden is flanked by members of the Old IRA and the United Ireland League as he reads the Proclaimation of the Republic as originally announced by Padraig Pearse at the GPO in Dublin in 1916. Below, a section of the huge crowd that thronged into Trafalgar Square for the event. According to Paddy Fahey's recollection, this photograph recorded only a small portion of the crowd on the day.

Tadgh Feehan, one of the 1916 Rising jubilee rally's organizers, in conversation with members of the Metropolitan Police. The event passed off without any disturbance.

Eddie Golden reading aloud the Proclamation. For many of his audience there was always the bitter-sweet knowledge that the Irish state which had its roots in the 1916 Rising was never sufficiently prosperous to offer a future to all its citizens.

Crowds waiting outside the Royal Albert Hall before the St Patrick's Day concert, 1965.

The flag is carried through the crowds that filled the Royal Albert Hall for a gala commemorative concert as part of the jubilee celebrations.

The Albert Hall had been used as a venue for Irish concerts since the 1930s, when an annual St Patrick's Day concert was held there. The event seen here took place in 1965.

The following historic photographs record events surrounding the IRA border campaign of 1959–61. The IRA launched an attack upon the Northern Irish border in that year. Unlike the 1939 campaign, the 1950s' campaign was not extended to the British mainland. This probably helped to mitigate the worst effects of anti-Irish feeling among the British population that was evinced in the 1970s. The government of the Republic collaborated with the British government and introduced internment for suspected republicans in the Republic. These photographs record protests against that policy by Irish republicans. Here a protest march is seen travelling down Oxford Street. The purpose of the march was to deliver a petition to the Irish Embassy.

Petitioners approach Grosvenor Place, the home of the Irish Embassy.

A civil rights protest on the Strand, 1969. A decade later, but the same questions remain. The border campaign of the late 1950s was unsuccessful and was finally called off by the IRA in 1962. By the late 1960s a new movement was beginning to emerge. Taking its lead from the civil disobedience movements in the USA, the civil rights movement began in Northern Ireland in 1967. Following the failure of the civil disobedience campaign, the IRA was revived in 1969/70.

The protesters enter Trafalgar Square, 1969.

A reception for Northern Irish Nationalist MPs held at the Irish Club, Eaton Square, 1964. This was soon after Wilson's victory, which promised to take Britain into the future with the white heat of technology. For Eddie McAteer, MP for Foyle 1953–69 (centre), and Nationalist Party leaders there was little in the way of opportunities for the majority of his nationalist constituents in the divided and gerrymandered Northern Irish state of the 1960s.

Ambassador Boland, Taoiseach Eamon De Valera and Frank Aiken, Minister of External Affairs, outside the Irish Embassy in London, 1960. At this stage in his career, De Valera had been Taoiseach for some twenty years and had moulded the south of Ireland in his likeness. Both De Valera and Aiken had fought against Britain in their youth, Aiken having been Chief of Staff of the Irregular Forces in 1923.

The guest of honour at the Monaghan Association dinner in 1969 was Erskine Childers. Childers was the son of the famous Irish rebel and author of *The Riddle of the Sands*. He was a Fianna Fail Tainiste and Minister for Health from 1969 to 1973. He became the third President of Ireland in 1973 and died in office, in 1975.

In 1964 the National University of Ireland hosted a gala St Patrick's Day reception for the Irish Taoiseach Sean Lemass. Like all the other Irish political figures of his generation, Lemass had fought in the Anglo-Irish War as a young man. He succeeded De Valera as Taoiseach in 1959, and is best remembered as presiding over the economic recovery that the country underwent in the 1960s. While he was Taoiseach there was a fall of 40 per cent in emigration from Ireland compared with its highest point in the early 1950s. It was Lemass who first applied to take Ireland into the EEC and who created a thaw in relations with the Northern Irish state. He died in 1971.

Another National University of Ireland banquet for St Patrick's Day, possibly 1963. Third from the right is Paddy Hillary TD, Minister of Education in the Fianna Fail government. Hillary distinguished himself at the Fianna Fail Ard Fheis in 1971, when he defended the party against the defectors Frank Boland and Neil Blaney. He was Irish Commissioner to the EEC from 1973 to 1976. He later became fifth President of Ireland after the resignation of Cearbhall O'Dalaigh in 1976.

The pipe-smoking Jack Lynch at the Cork Association dinner, 1965. Lynch was famous for holding six All-Ireland medals for hurling and one for football in the 1940s. He became Taoiseach following Sean Lemass's resignation in 1966. His administration epitomized the new Ireland of the 1960s. He was in office from 1966 to 1973 and again from 1977 to 1979.

Bobby Molloy, Minister of Defence in the Fianna Fail government of Jack Lynch stepping it out with Julie Brook of the Ted Kavanagh Troupe of Irish dancers at the Galway Association dinner dance, 1969. Molloy was one of the famous mohair-suited young Fianna Fail TDs of the period. From the dizziness of the dance floor Molloy would soon become embroiled in the famous arms trial of 1970.

Senator Gus Healey, Lord Mayor of Cork, and the Lady Mayoress at St George's Cathedral, Southwark, before the Terence MacSwiney memorial mass, 1964. Also in the photograph are: Frank McCabe, national organizer of the United Irish Association, Tadgh Feehan (third left) and Frank Lee of the Old IRA (fourth right). Terence MacSwiney, the Mayor of Cork, died in Brixton Prison in 1920 following a hunger strike which lasted seventy-four days.

The St Patrick's Day banquet hosted by the National University of Ireland in London, 1959. One of Ireland's best-known elder statesmen of the era was present, Sean MacEntee (right). At that time MacEntee was Minister of Health in the Fianna Fail Government and later Tainiste. Also in the photograph (right to left) are Michael McCormack, President of the NUI Club, Mrs McCann, Hugh McCann, the Irish Ambassador, and Mrs McEntee.

Bill Norton, former leader of the Irish Labour Party, on a visit to the Irish Club in Camden, 1962. Mr Norton, who had served as Tainiste in the two inter-party governments of the 1950s, is seen here in the kitchens with Tom McGowan and Fr Dowling. We do not know the names of the women workers.

These two photographs, although not associated with the Irish community, are historic in their own right. Paddy Fahey never forgot that he was a press photographer and when a story presented itself he took it up. These photographs were taken in 1962 when Oswald Mosley held a rally near Paddy's studio at Ridley Road in Dalston. Mosley's Union Movement re-established itself after the Second World War and caused great controversy by campaigning against immigration from the New Commonwealth. While the movement was not targeted at Irish people in the way that it was against others, anti-Irish prejudice was also a fact of everyday life at the time. However, it was not until the 1970s and '80s that radical Irish Londoners sought to find cause with other ethnic minorities.

WHEN IRISH EYES ARE SMILING

This evocative photograph is Paddy Fahey at his best. The date and the event are unknown, but if anyone recognizes the people or recalls the event please contact the Grange Museum or Cricklewood Archive.

Irish Londoners of the 1950s and '60s had a difficult life away from home and while families worked hard they were often marginalized by mainstream British society. Yet when one looks at these photographs by Paddy Fahey one is also reminded that this was a community of people who made their own way, relied on themselves, contributed greatly to the physical character of London and never lost their informality, friendliness and essential good nature. This collection of images is included as a fitting reminder of the contribution both of the Irish community and of Paddy Fahey individually to the development of modern London.

On their return from an outing to Clacton-on-Sea this group of Pioneers stop and dance a Siege of Ennis at the roadside, 1961. This evocative photograph is one of Paddy's best: the photographer is not on the outside looking in, he is one of the people observing his own. If any photograph sums up the vibrancy and self-reliance of Irish Londoners in the 1950s and '60s then this must be the one. The outing was organized by the Church of the Sacred Heart, Quex Road, Kilburn.

The dancehall was where Paddy's skill came most into play. He was always able to catch people at just the right moment. Here mineral-bar staff pose for a photograph. The venue may be the Galtymore and the year is probably 1965.

A holiday photograph of Peggy Fahey's family, Waterford, 1957. Peggy's mother is at the front on the right.

This lovely photograph was taken at the Tipperarymen's Association dinner dance, 1961. The clothes, the cigarette and the general demeanour of the unknown subjects come from an innocent age.

The 1965 Waterford Association dinner dance was obviously a jolly affair. The picture tells it all.

The novelist Edna O'Brien attended the Sugawn Theatre's 1975 production of *Finnegan's Wake*.

In 1964 the Mayo Association held a function at the Camden Irish Centre. This captures the essence of any of the hundreds of events covered by Paddy, best bib and tucker and enjoying the show.

A Limerick Association outing to Southampton, 1955. It is arguably Paddy Fahey's best surviving photograph.

In 1957 Paddy, his wife Peggy and their family went home to Ireland for their summer holiday. Needless to say he took along his camera. In Paddy's photographic diary he records the images from that trip simply as holiday snaps. Yet these snaps are also a document of the time. Going home, staying with relatives and helping with the harvest was very much part of life for many of the London Irish. This photograph features their young son Patrick and his grandfather.

Rinty Monaghan, godfather at a christening in
Deptford, 1961. Rinty was a world-champion
boxer and a familiar figure to the Irish community.

Nurses often appear in Paddy's photographs. They are unfortunately the only Irish workers that regularly
feature in his work. Paddy seems to have had a great rapport with his clients and this comes across very
well in this 1955 group photograph taken at St Joseph's Hospice, Hackney.

IN PADDY'S FOOTSTEPS

*Paddy Fahey holding his son Patrick in his arms in
Wexford, 1957. Sadly Patrick died while a young man.*

Paddy Fahey was not the only photographer to take photographs of the Irish community. From within the community itself men like Gerry Harrington and Martin Moroney were well known and also recorded a huge number of events. However, Paddy was taking photographs from an earlier time and for a longer period than anyone else. Towards the end of his career in particular local newspapers in London began to recognize the need for producing material of interest to the Irish community. The following images are taken from the photo archive of the *Willesden Chronicle*, and are housed at Cricklewood Library and Archive. They are mainly the work of the the the late Bob Clegg, a staff photographer at the paper.

Sinking foundations for a twelve-storey block of flats, Kilburn Square, 1961. We do not positively know that this is an Irish crew but it would be extraordinary if it were not. In the decades following the Second World War it was Irishmen who took on the major burden of rebuilding the capital.

On 23 February 1968 Mick Meaney, a Kilburn barman, was buried alive under the Admiral Nelson in Malvern Mews, Kilburn. He was attempting to break the world record for live burial. His manager was the famous Butty Sugrue, proprietor of the Admiral Nelson. Mick stayed underground for sixty-one days. Here Mick is lowered into his grave. His doctor had organized a thousand calorie a day diet for him while underground. That probably didn't include the bottles of stout passed down by visitors during his ordeal!

Sixty-one days after he was buried eight Irishmen, supervised by Butty Sugrue, began to dig Mick up. After fifteen minutes Butty shouted, 'we have him lads' and Mick emerged once again into the air.

Hundreds of people watched as Mick and his coffin were hoisted on to the back of a 10-ton tipper truck and driven all round Kilburn. Diana Dors and the bantamweight boxer Alan Rudkin were among the crowd, along with TV cameras from the BBC.

Paddy Fahey claimed that he left press photography following the escalation of violence in Ireland in the 1970s and the British bombing campaign. The press coverage of the London Irish in these years was often quite grim. One can understand why Paddy left its coverage to a new generation of press photographer. This march along the Cricklewood Broadway occurred in October 1971.

Kilburn High Road. The march began outside the Crown in Cricklewood and ended in Hyde Park. It was organized by the Anti-Internment League to protest against the introduction of internment in Northern Ireland.

Bernadette Devlin, as she was then known, addresses an anti-internment meeting at Kilburn Square, October 1971. Bernadette was the youngest ever woman MP in the British Parliament.